Visita el mercado en primavera, verano, otoño e invierno. ¿Cuántas frutas y verduras distintas puedes encontrar? Utiliza las **pistas visuales** en cada página.

Squash
$1.39/lb

kohlrabi
colirrábano

watermelon
sandía

Spring

romaine lettuce
lechuga romana

asparagus
espárragos

snow peas
chícharos chinos

rhubarb ruibarbo

carrot
zanahoria

mushrooms
champiñones

Butter Lettuce $.99 each

Radishes $1.39/bunch

butter lettuce
lechuga francesa

apricots
albaricoques

jicama
jícama

radish
rábano

garlic ajo

broccoli brócoli

collard greens

berza

green beans

habichuelas verdes

strawberry fresa

Honeydew $2.39 each

blood orange

naranja roja

avocado aguacate

honeydew melon melón chino

Summer

peach
melocotón

loquats
nísperos

lychees
lichis

beet
remolachas

mango
mango

kiwi
kiwi

tomato
tomate

Mango
$1.50 each

Artichoke
$1.99 each

peppers
pimientos

plums
ciruelas

artichokes
alcachofas

kohlrabi
colirrábano

grapes

figs
higos

uvas

onion
cebolla

leeks
puerros

jalapeños
jalapeños

okra
quingombó

radish
rábano

Figs
$2.59/lb

eggplant
berenjena

watermelon
sandía

honeydew
melon

melón chino

potato
papa

Fall

parsnips
chirivías

persimmons
caquis

pear
pera

cabbage
repollo

cauliflower
coliflor

apple
manzana

Persimmons
3 for $5.00

Cranberries
$2.49/lb

rutabaga
colinabo

pumpkin
calabaza

cranberries
arándanos rojos

broccoli
brócoli

quinces
membrillos

Brussels sprouts
coles de Bruselas

beet
remolacha

Swiss chard
acelga

acorn squash
calabaza bellota

Quinces
$1.99/lb

Sweet Potato
$.79/lb

kohlrabi
colirrábano

sweet potato

camote

celery root

apio nabo

Winter

star fruit
carambola

cabbage
repollo

pear
pera

navel orange
naranja de
ombligo

**kabocha
squash**
calabaza
kabocha

celery root
apio nabo

pomegranate
granada

Kabocha
$3 each

Celery Root
$2.50/lb

sunchokes
tupinambo

onion
cebolla

**delicata
squash**

**calabaza
delicata**